MAI ALLEN was born in Ireland before emigrating. She wondered why we are here and what we are meant to do.

Finding that thoughts accompanied with visualisation could overcome challenges, she wanted to write and help people who were faced with problems. She now lives with her husband in a suburb of Melbourne.

To Shannon,

with Love

To Shannon, with Love

Mai Allen

ATHENA PRESS
LONDON

TO SHANNON, WITH LOVE

ISBN: 978 1 84748 357 7

First published 2008 by
ATHENA PRESS
Queen's House, 2 Holly Road
Twickenham TW1 4EG
United Kingdom

Printed for Athena Press

Dedicated to my grandchildren:
Kris, Danny, Jaymie, Kian, Shannon, Mitchell, Joshua, Rhys,
Amy, Tristan and Rory.
And to all the grandchildren of the world.
Go in peace…

My first grandchild! When I was told this news by the travellers I was over the moon. They didn't know whether you were a girl or boy. To me that matters little. You live far away in the west, but that is your path. Fathers and mothers are there to nurture and protect, but grandparents are there to provide answers to questions that parents may be too busy to deliver.

What questions would you ask me if you were here? To know this I looked at the children and young people around me. I even searched the foreign newspapers. I will write my answers to these questions as though I were beside you and you could hear my voice. Some day perhaps, and I hope it is not too late, you may come in search of your roots and find this response. As you will be educated in Western culture I have to delve into it for the universal answers.

You may say, 'Old one, why bother?' My reply is that in newspapers, television and radio reports and even in the common talk of the people today, everything appears negative and fear is rampant over the world. Life in the future appears very grey and we don't know what lies ahead. We feel the world heating up. We are told varieties of wildlife are disappearing, with some on the verge of extinction. In one place, water disappears, causing food shortages. Floods wreak havoc in another region and people lose lives, houses and land. Wars abound and health problems surface right, left and centre. These are world problems which can depress you if you face them alone. You may try to escape facing them through drink or drugs or both. These things help in the short term but later present further problems. Later those who are really low can invite the permanent solution to a problem – suicide! If you were here with me now, child, you would ask, 'Who made this? And who made that?' And I would answer, 'God.' Then, like all the other children around, you would ask, 'Who is God?' and 'Why are things made?' Science, which you will be familiar with later, says our universe came into being through a 'bang'.

Every time I hear a very loud bang, I chuckle and say, 'Has God created another universe?' Scientists are, however, trying hard to find the answer. As to the reason why mankind was created, at present they haven't a clue. At this moment in the Western world one has to look to the Bible for reasons.

You may find that some people treat the Bible with superstitious awe and believe it literally. The Old and New Testaments are filled with ideas and views of different people. Archaeologists inform us that these stories, oral at the beginning, were written down many decades after the events took place. Scribes could add their own views or that of their employers. Translators could make many errors. We are told that, 'It is easier for a camel to go through the eye of a needle than for a rich man to enter the kingdom of God.' In Aramaic the word '*gamla*' is alike for camel and rope. As Jesus said this while he was talking to his disciples who had formerly been fishermen, it makes more sense that he was talking about rope. They were used to taking needles and cord to mend their nets, and rope would have been even stronger! (See Matthew 19:24).

You, child, must therefore read the Bible using your intuition. Get a feeling that, 'Yes this makes sense', or 'No, that is nonsense!' Thinking in ages past was very different to how we think today, so knowledge of the background and customs of those in the Bible proves helpful. See *Idioms in the Bible Explained* by George M Lamsa. This little book also throws light on what appears to be Jesus' indifference to the death of a disciple's father and his last words on the cross.

Let us now look at the first chapter of the book of Genesis where we meet the originator of Earth called God. As men in that society were considered more worthy than women, this God is specified as male. We will visit this later. Genesis informs us that God is a creator. He looks out at first and sees just empty space and through sound creates the universe.

Later, he creates mankind in his image and likeness. You only have to look around to see how diverse humanity is in sex and race. The only effects we have in common are the basic elements of our physical bodies, i.e. atoms, cells, electrons etc. Therefore, God must be some type of force field comprising all these elements. Also, one cannot create something from nothing. Scientists tell us that empty space as we know it is not vacant. It is comprised of all sorts of visible and invisible elements. This means that God (the force field) occupied all space and so created, from within himself, our universe. This would explain the verse in the Bible, 'In him we live and move and have our being' (Acts 17:28). Everything on Earth is born, breathes, lives and dies. This includes animals, fish, birds, vegetation and minerals. On dying they go back to form basic matter. Humans were created last and given dominion over everything created previously.

God, the creator, the force field, we will now call the 'Great Spirit'. We are primarily spirits and not created but are a part of the Great Spirit, and are therefore eternal and never die. Let me help you understand, child, by giving you an example. You are beside the sea. Take one little drop of water and place it in the middle of your hand. Doesn't it look small, lonely and different from the vast expanse of water? And yet it is still the same and part of the whole.

At first, spirit was like the angels and very obedient. We brought all the attributes of our source with us – love, light, beauty and harmony. We lived in a finer ether or sphere where we could think and create quickly. We were, however, like children, pure and naive. The Great Spirit wants us to be wise in handling any situation. To be like this we needed patience, tolerance, love, faith and divine understanding, so the Great Spirit then sent us to Earth in order to evolve and grow in these qualities.

Earth is comprised of grosser, heavier materials and therefore the spirit needs a physical body in which to live and function in. We are required to remain with this body for a certain time limit, so the spirit is joined to it by a cord. The physical body requires a renewal of energy and therefore rests daily during a period of sleep. This body could not rest and recuperate if the spirit was conscious in it so the spirit leaves but remains attached by the cord (Ecc. 12:6). This physical body we call the 'ego' appears lifeless without the spirit, as when we are sleeping or unconscious. We call this spirit the 'higher self'. When the higher self returns and we awake, it animates the body. We become aware of our surroundings and can move and speak. Those people who have had an out-of-body experience can confirm that the human body is motionless (although living and breathing) when the higher self breaks free or flows out of it. You can look down from any vantage point and view your own body as a separate entity.

The Great Spirit gave mankind the gift of free will. He stood back and allowed us to evolve at our own rate. The Great Spirit does not interfere in our lives, or the gift of free will would be void. The Great Spirit is therefore 'impersonal'. So, child, know that you are an ageless spirit inhabiting a human body and given a name while you are here. The human body is born, lives, learns and dies, but you – the spirit – live on. To people on Earth, Abraham, Isaac, and Jacob were dead, but Jesus told the Sadducees that God (the Great Spirit) had said, 'I am the God of Abraham, Isaac and Jacob. He is not God of the dead but of the living' (Matthew 22:32).

The Great Spirit creates and so we create also. How? Through our mind, our imagination and how we visualise things. 'Keep your heart [what you strive for – what you visualise] with all vigilance for out of it are the issues of life.' (Prov. 4:23).

When you arrive on Earth you are deprived of the conscious memory of the heaven worlds; otherwise you would be homesick and wouldn't wish to remain on Earth. As Earth life is made of grosser matter, it takes longer for you to visualise and experience the results. You may become frustrated and caught up with others and imagine all the wrong sorts of things. If this went to extremes, mankind could exterminate itself. The Great Spirit made allowance for this and added the law of cause and effect. To develop spiritually we need to learn discrimination. You don't really appreciate the pleasures of heaven until you have been through the worst possible fear and torment.

Earth is a planet of duality, of love and hate, bitter and sweet, good and bad. Free will then allows us to love or hate and gives us a future filled with abundance or lack. With the law of cause and effect we can be selfish, cruel, dominate, or even murder others and our acts will rebound on us. In the Bible we find 'An eye for an eye' (Matthew 5:38) and 'All who take swords will die by swords' (Matthew 26:52). If instead we are kind and do helpful acts to others, we in turn will be helped. 'Whatever you wish men to do for you do likewise also for them: for this is the law and the prophets' (Matthew 7:12).

Over a period of time the working out of this law upon our person will instil us with knowledge. We are like children and only learn through our mistakes. Child, you may sometime be told not to touch a hot stove as it will burn you. If you forget, or are stubborn and touch it, you will be burnt. Finally, after a series of burns, which only hurt you and no one else, the message gets through and you learn that this is a foolish act. You won't do it again. You have learnt knowledge.

Full knowledge of all qualities corresponding to wisdom cannot be achieved in one lifetime; therefore you must come back again and again to earth to learn further lessons. Any crimes committed earlier have to be paid for and you may have missed the opportunity to do so in an earlier life. Reincarnation is the belief that the spirit after death returns to a new body (not always immediately – periods can differ). Some of the early Church leaders wanted to get rid of the knowledge of reincarnations and had it omitted from the Bible. Nevertheless it was unwittingly left in: 'And as Jesus passed by he saw a man who was blind from his mother's womb. And his disciples asked him, saying, "Teacher, who did sin, this man or his parents that he was born blind?" ' (John 9:2).

If Jesus had not believed in reincarnation he would have ridiculed his followers at this point. Later on, he himself quizzed his disciples, ' "What do the people say concerning me that I am?" ' They answer, ' "John the Baptist or Elijah or one of the old prophets" ' (Luke 9:18–19) At another time Jesus said, 'For all the prophets and the law prophesised until John – and if you wish to accept it he is Elijah who was to come.' (Matthew 11:13–14), meaning John the Baptist had been Elijah the prophet in a past incarnation.

Before incarnation on earth, you in spirit form meet a group of wise elders who advise and give you your assignment for the coming life here. Your higher self is enthusiastic, you accept and so the day and hour of your birth is planned. You are anaesthetised to allow you to forget the wonders of heaven and enter Earth life with a fresh perspective. As a baby on Earth you arrive lacking anything materialistic. Inwardly, however, various traits, faults and gifts accumulated from previous lives are stored. These will surface as you mature to be helped or hindered by the present life. You must develop balance, patience, tolerance, universal love and wisdom and therefore will discover yourself in differing situations: you may be rich or poor, male or female, healthy or diseased. You will be one of the five races – black, brown, white, yellow, red – or a mixture of these. Your birth can take place anywhere on earth. The outcome of good or bad situations in earlier lives may have to be worked on in the present chosen life. You may now find yourself with parents, siblings, friends who were friends or enemies previously. Your mother now might have been a prior employee; your sister, a niece; your brother, a fellow worker; your friend, a former brother. A splendid opportunity lies before you to enhance friendships and make them closer. Enmity can be overcome and changed into love or at least the beginning of friendship. In each life you will be required to enter a fresh, different role. Shakespeare, open to inspiration, wrote, 'All the world's a stage, and all the men and women merely players' (*As You Like It,* Act II, Scene VII, lines 139–166).

Most people (there are a few exceptions – see Dr Ian Stevenson's *The Evidence for Survival from Claimed Memories of Former Incarnations*) totally forget their previous lives, which makes it smoother for them to start anew. The sobering effect of this, however, is that some may also forget how strong and capable they are in spirit. The spheres of the spirit world and Earth are not areas set apart but intertwine each other. I'll give you an example: you are walking through a wood on a bright sunny day. A gentle breeze brings a waft of jasmine from the perfumed flowers growing ahead. Before that, you were only conscious of tree smells, grass and bracken. These perfumes all mingle together, you can't tell where one starts and one finishes. This is similar to how the eternal realm interpenetrates the earth. Those who inhabit the spiritual world are composed of finer substance (like ourselves when in spirit form). The Great Spirit, knowing that we would need help from time to time, has allowed us to be provided this service from these inhabitants of the spirit world. The best known are archangels and angels. On most occasions they cannot interfere in the impending events in people's lives. They don't possess free will so it is up to us to ask them for help when we require it. They are pure in spirit and only too pleased to offer us love, healing and protection. St Peter is helped and released from prison by an angel in the Bible (Acts 12:6–11). All the apostles imprisoned are liberated by an angel (Acts 5:18–19); Jesus underwent a period of temptation, and when this was ended the angels came and assisted him (Mark 1:12).

Family members or friends who have died or higher spiritual persons can also help: 'And though the Lord give you the bread of adversity and the water of affliction yet you shall see your teacher and your ears shall hear a word behind you saying, "This is the way. Walk in it when you turn to the right or when you turn to the left." ' (Isaiah 30:20–21).

We as humans possess an elemental flesh body, a brain which receives and sends out messages and a system which works to keep the body alive automatically. This body we will call the ego. If the human knows nothing about the spirit (the higher self) inhabiting it, then it believes the body is all that there is. In times of peril or great pain, mankind, feeling separate and alone, has called to the god he worships for assistance. Others maybe with a religious leaning or a wish within for better things would also pray to their god for whatever is required. It is of no avail praying to the Great Spirit. He has given you free will. He already knows you are perfect. The Great Spirit is timeless. On Earth, on the other hand, we are under the illusion of time and evolve slowly. The Jews remonstrated with Jesus, accusing him of blaspheming. They told him he was only a man yet made himself God. He had said, 'I and my father are of one accord.' He answered them, 'Is it not so written in your law – "I said you were gods?" ' (John 10:30–34). He meant that Jesus, the human body (the ego) and the father (the spirit, the higher self) were of one accord, the ego performing the will of the higher self obediently. Jesus the teacher told us to pray to our higher self – our spirit who animates the human body. He called it our father and defined the difference in it from the Great Spirit (which is everywhere) by saying 'which is in heaven'.

Let us look at the prayer and its meaning:

> Our father which art in heaven.
> Hallowed be thy name.
> Thy kingdom come, thy will be done as in heaven so in earth.
> Give us bread for our needs from day to day,
> And forgive us our offences as we have forgiven our offenders.
> Do not let us enter into temptation but deliver us from evil, For thine is the kingdom and the glory for ever and ever.
> Amen.
>
> Luke 11:2–4 in:
> *Holy Bible from the Ancient Eastern Text*

The meaning of the prayer, child, is:

> Our higher self in heaven,
> May your name be sacred.
> Let all be harmony here.

May I surrender and do your will here likewise to that done in heaven.
Give us instruction from day to day.
May we be treated in the same manner by which we treat others.
Don't let us be tempted into doing that which is not right and extract us from morally wrong situations.
For yours is the spiritual realm, the influential authority and the state of harmony which is eternal.
Amen.

When Moses asked the name of God he was told, 'I am who I am' (Ex. 3:14); a strange name until you realise that when each of us says it, we vocalise and acknowledge bringing the higher self into the physical body. It is written, 'You shall not take the Lord your God in vain [to curse it] for the Lord will not hold him guiltless who takes his name in vain' (Deut. 5:11). This is and has through the ages been thought to mean saying something bad about God, Jesus or the holy family. What it actually means is saying something disparaging about your higher self – the spirit which is part of the Great Spirit and animates your physical body. Examples: people may say, I am a worm, I am worthless, I am a nobody. Jesus said, 'For by your words you shall be justified [in the right] and by your words you shall be found guilty' (Matthew 12:37).

In the Bible we find the name Satan, the devil, the chief adversary of God. Satan reigns over hell. The Great Spirit who created the universe out of himself is all love, light and harmony and therefore cannot create an adversary. There is only the 'one' so we cannot have two in life.

As an extreme example, imagine a man. He was rich

with much authority and abused this and was cruel to subordinates and died without making remission for his deeds. In his next incarnation his nature is unchanged but he is disadvantaged. Everything that can go wrong does so, making him jealous, angry, bitter and malicious. This builds up an aura or force field of negativity around him. As more and more people have felt likewise over the ages this field of negativity has grown and covered a certain part of our planet.

We possess a brain which receives and broadcasts thoughts. Early man supposed the body was all that they possessed and felt isolated and alone. This led him to be terrified in certain circumstances. This fear became personified in their thoughts as a god – an evil one, the opposite to the Great Spirit and called Satan. Satan is a thought form; it is error, self-deception, misguidance and wrongdoing.

Let's look at some examples of this: when Jesus informs the disciples about his coming crucifixion, Peter says, 'God forbid lord, this shall never happen to you.' Jesus answered, 'Get behind me Satan, you are a hindrance to me for you are not on the side of God but of men' (Matt. 16:22–23). This means, 'Peter, take your wrong thoughts out of my sight. They hold me back because they are not spiritual but physical.'

Jesus, in order to find out if he is capable of going the right way, fasts for forty days. While his physical body is in this fragile psychological state, his ego reflects on how wonderful the powers he possesses could be, how influential great earthly authority is, how he could be omnipotent by himself alone and he could even leap off high buildings and angels would catch him. Jesus faced all these images and thoughts one by one striking them off and declaring them false, deceptive and all errors (Luke 4:1–13).

Where now and what is hell?

Jesus said, 'In my father's house are many rooms. If it were not so, I would have told you. I go to prepare a place for you' (John 14:2). He later tells a malefactor crucified with him that he would join him in paradise that day (See Luke 23:43). Jesus had also earlier recounted the story about the rich man who was selfish and who was tormented after death when in hell (See Luke 16:19–25).

Hell is known as a place of suffering, darkness and gloom. You ask me, child, 'Why would the Great Spirit create a hell?' Ask yourself, would that which is universal love, purity and goodness even want to create a hell? No! It was mankind, through the error of imagination wrongly used, who created this area of darkness which, over aeons of time, solidified and became blacker and blacker. Into its sphere are drawn those spirits of similar aspect. Scientists will inform you that like attracts like. An old saying reinforces this: 'Birds of a feather flock together'. Paradise then is that sphere of light, love and harmony into which are assembled like-minded spirits. Hell is lower down in the sphere, descending from dimness to impenetrable blackness and attracting its own inhabitants also. Over differing periods of time the thoughts of these inhabitants will become clearer, affording them elevation to a brighter level. At some future date they will return to earth to discharge their wrongful actions and uplift themselves. Jesus tells us, 'There will be such joy before the angels of God over one sinner who repents' (Luke 15:10). This means there is joy over a wrongdoer whose way of thinking is changed. Once you have learnt all your lessons on Earth there is no need to return. 'He who overcomes, I will make a pillar in the temple of my God and he shall not go out again (Rev 3:12).

The spirit who, while in physical body, finally gains wisdom, universal love and enlightenment is now of strong character with no further need to go out and reincarnate on Earth again. Jesus the physical man was tempted many times, just like you, but he remained true. He was faultless, loving and pure-minded. He was anointed, receiving the highest of spiritual initiations. He was 'Christed' – acknowledged by the Great Spirit as having discovered and reclaimed his source, and John bore witness: 'I saw the spirit descend as a dove from heaven and it remained on him' (John 1:32).

'The Christ' is a spiritual title. Jesus was about to perform what most regard as miracles, such as healing, controlling the elements, expanding small amounts into plenty, appearing and disappearing at will, but he was also pure, enlightened and loving – there are fakirs and other people in the world today who can perform many seemingly miraculous acts without being spiritual in any way. He was the ultimate teacher. He came to demonstrate how life should be lived and what we should do or say. He declared, 'I am the way, the truth and the life; no one comes to the father, but by me. If you had known me you would have known my father also: Henceforth you know him and have seen him' (John 14:6–7), meaning: I am the way you should live, the true and eternal life and you ascend spiritually through living this way.

Jesus set the example and we can follow the father. St Paul wrote in short for us to do everything in devotion to God, to give no offence to different races or religions. He said he tried to please everyone, not to gain for himself but that they might be rescued. He added, 'Be imitators of me as I am of Christ' (1 Cor. 10:31–33 and 11:1). Jesus our teacher has promised us: 'Truly, truly, I say to you, he who believes in me will also do the works that I do, and greater works than these will he do, because I go to the father. Whatsoever you ask in my name, I will do it that the father will be glorified in the son. If you ask anything in my name I will do it' (John 14:12–14) – i.e. in the name of the Christ. Jesus has shown us the way to live and if we follow his example we shall rise in consciousness and in purity of body – the flesh and the spirit being equal. The ego willingly obeys the higher self; the two are now one. The Christ is universal love and we shall now be 'Christed'. We are the prodigal son at last acknowledging and knowing the Great Spirit.

Satan is one adversary of the Great Spirit; another is money. Money is primarily just an item of exchange. You earn or are given it. You can barter easily with those people in your locality but when travelling long distances money is a lighter commodity to carry and may be used in the same capacity as items of trade. Most people today live a different lifestyle from those in the past ages and money is now a requirement for nearly everyone. It provides you with food, drink, clothing, housing, transport, education or enjoyment, for example, sports or arts. Whereas in earlier cultures people tended to be jealous of others having lands and extensive herds of cattle, nowadays money has taken this position; it is assigned more power than it necessitates.

Jesus understood this and told us, 'No man can serve two masters for either he will hate the one and like the other or he will honour one and despise the other. You cannot serve God and money' (Matt. 6:24). In other words, you can't love both equally. Religious thoughts, views and sermons throughout the ages have given the idea that money is to be shunned – not by those in authority, but by the populace at large. History has proved that the uneducated and poor can be led more readily by those in authority who can control their thoughts and actions.

Possessing money is not a crime, it is your treatment of it that makes it either valuable or a hindrance. St Paul said, 'For the love of money is the root of all evils – it is through this craving that some have wandered away from the faith and pierced their hearts with many pangs' (1 Tim 6:10).

The Great Spirit wants all good for you: 'Put me to the test,' says the Lord of Hosts, 'if I will not open the window of heaven for you and pour down for you an overflowing blessing' (Mal 3:10).

Money is simply there for use. It is neither to be worshipped or shunned. If you have too much then help those less fortunate. Don't hoard it. Don't puff yourself up by saying you have more of it than anyone else, for you give it too much power and so attract thieves, criminals and jealous acquaintances. Put it in its place and enjoy it for its exchange rate only.

Different areas of life on Earth can afford precious lessons. These interests are only wrong when they become addictive and lead us not only to hurt our physical body but maybe to cause harm to others. These harmful interests may include gambling, drinking, smoking and drugs.

People are diverse in their ideas, emotions and body make-up. One person is satisfied with a small meal; another has to gorge until sick. One will enjoy a pleasant glass of alcohol with a meal; another will deprive his family of finances to drink himself into oblivion. Drugs appear to star above all other vices. Life itself appears hard to you and drugs tempt you by telling you, *take this cannabis, it's cheap and easy to acquire. On smoking it you may feel drowsy – but isn't that good! You can now drift with life and be happy. There are no high barriers around you.*

Of course not! The sharpness of your intellect has become blunted in smoking these leaves. Whereas before it was possible for you to attempt and master physics, in a decade or less you have been demoted to higher mathematics.

This downward arc can continue blunting the sharpness of the intellect even more. A little later, someone may say to you, 'Try heroin, it gives a bigger high.' Well apparently that is very true – at least for that first time. You take the heroin and you reach a state of ecstasy that you can't believe. You want that feeling again but no matter what you do or how much you take you never reach it! Meanwhile you have found it's a very expensive, addictive practice. It's also an insidious habit which controls your thoughts, emotions and actions. You are its slave and you will now lie, steal and even kill for it. Your ego is under its sway and unless the higher self can let in a ray of light before it's too late your physical body will end up dead. With enlightenment you may seek help to overcome the dependency on drugs. People are always around to give aid when required.

Peer pressure can also extend into sex. Sex of itself is not sinful; however, it should be the happy union in two people who love each other. When it is sought obsessively or for money then it causes problems. Where does it hit most? In your consciousness. St Paul wrote, 'The body is not meant for immorality but for the Lord,' and 'Every other sin a man commits is outside the body but the immoral man sins against his own body.' Your body is a temple of the Holy Spirit within you in which you have found God. So glorify God in your body' (See: 1 Cor. 6:12–20).

Disease can appear in the body through many differing ways. It could be an illness passed on via the family. It could be from air, food, water or human contact. It could be attracted even by fear-filled thoughts. Negative thoughts can precede similar actions, for example, irritation, anger or hate. The law of cause and effect will then take over and in its time the action will recoil on the perpetrator.

This may be in the form of some disease attacking the ego. A paralysed man was carried in on his bed before Jesus, who looked at him said, 'Man, your sins are forgiven you.' The surrounding scribes and Pharisees asked, 'Who is this that speaks blasphemies? Who can forgive sins but God only?' Jesus answered them, 'Which is easier to say, "Your sins are forgiven you," or to say, "Rise and walk?" ' He added, 'Know that the son of man has authority on earth to forgive sins.' The paralytic was healed. (See Luke 5:18–25).

Jesus who had been Christed had many powerful gifts, one of which was the ability to see a person's thoughts. In the case of the paralytic he realised the man had overcome that area of negativity which had eventually led to the paralysis. Now that the person was more positive, his faith allowed Jesus to firmly stamp this fact in his consciousness.

When you know deep inside and without doubt that a certain thought or action is very wrong, and that you will never ever act that way again or entertain that thought, then the law of cause and effect alters. The effect dissolves. This will not happen by merely vocalising it, however. No! It will only occur when contrition floods your consciousness and you see and face the cause, and know finally you will never do it again – it has become foreign to your character.

Disease contains lessons in itself. You may have come here in order to experience the drawbacks of a certain illness. Does it leave you friendless and isolated? After the initial anger followed by depression, do you now need to build up patience? Maybe you have been overwhelmed by the compassion, love and help of friends and strangers. They have given you all and more. This could instil in you a strong faith in the innate kindness of the human race. Whatever you learn in life has purpose. It could be for your own use, it could be meant to help another. Share your knowledge, because nature abhors a vacuum. You will find that as you share ideas with one person, another will come along and dispense concepts you require. Never consider any job menial, downgrading or disagreeable. You have chosen that work for some reason so don't attach negative thoughts to it. Instead, treat it as though it is the most valuable, worthwhile, pleasurable job on earth. Like attracts like. Either the surroundings of your work will change for the better or you will find yourself with a more agreeable position.

So child, what I have tried to tell you is I believe that there is a Great Spirit which we and all things in, on and around the earth and within the universe are part of. This Great Spirit has disclosed that in making mankind in its image; it is both male and female and so both are equal in the higher self. Spirit therefore is androgynous.

The ego, on being given free will, made prayer to the Great Spirit unnecessary. The law of cause and effect, bringing pain or pleasure, distils knowledge finally. As this cannot be worked out in one lifetime, many lifetimes are required. The ego senses that it has left something better in order to experience life on Earth and can be filled with apprehension or fear at times. Prayer to the higher self for guidance and help in avoiding the pitfalls of life can instil courage and faith, and calls for support from angels and archangels will not go unheeded.

If you have come to earth in a male body it's because you have to act out a masculine role in this lifetime and if you are a female then vice versa. Therefore in whatever role you play, respect the other gender. The same goes for race and colour. How can you in your race and colour today look down on and despise another, when you possibly were one of them yourself, perhaps only two or three lifetimes ago? This adds another dimension making it foolish to look down upon, restrict or try to dominate races or sexes. Just think, you may be heading off to war and killing your great-grandchildren! The law of cause and effect rebounds on countries also. Therefore when a country goes to war and uses weapons to kill people, in time, war will be waged against it. If you are rich, don't waste the opportunity to do good with your education or money. If you are high-born, cultivate tolerance.

Whatever religion you find yourself in, meditate and find the love and light within it. All great world religions have a golden thread connecting them one to another. That way which you have chosen is to give you research into spirituality in this life. Don't regard others as incorrect. Avoid being a fundamentalist and pushing your views down people's throats. Just think that if the Great Spirit had wanted only one sex, colour and religion then only one person would have been required. No. For some reason The Great Spirit appears to request diversity in all matters.

Earth life reminds me somewhat of the path of a tornado. Visualise an area of land with towns, buildings, people and cattle. A tornado passes through. Everything is altered and changed. People, if filled with a loftier ideal, can replace it all with better layout of towns and excellent housing etc. This can hold until maybe decades later a tornado strikes again, but while it is the outside of the tornado that causes havoc and change, the inside is calm, still, immovable – just like the experiences that hit parts of earth at times on the physical outer area. Inside, the Great Spirit remains untouched – the same yesterday, today and tomorrow.

Another example is to picture a diamond ring with all its beautiful flawless facets. Each faces a different angle. Every surface catches light in various ways yet these facets are all connected, part of the whole yet one in substance. The diamond is the Great Spirit, the facets are ourselves – the spirits.

Marriage and partnership is the coming together of two people. In this lifetime, child, will you marry or not? You could remain single with a focus on your vocation or other area in life. Whether married or single you could be childless; either by choice or circumstances. There are differing reasons for being childless, in this life you may not require parenting skills. You may have gotten rid of unwanted children before and now experience the pangs of not having any. You might even have produced a large family in a previous life. Everyone is different. The union through marriage or partnership can be based on love, lust, money, guilt or many other reasons. Some may even be forced to marry through family problems or dominance.

Negative people attract similar qualities in a new partner. You and your helpmate have either come together to join in a combined effort to establish something in life or solve problems initiated in an earlier lifetime. Either way you are not here to criticise, dominate or hurt the other. Besides, the tendencies you criticise in another are usually latent within yourself and need to be brought out and worked on.

Why should you even try to dominate another? You will never ever agree one hundred per cent because you are two individuals with different backgrounds, pasts and future ideals. It's better to listen to each other's point of view – you may even benefit from this. In the case of violence, only the offender, in facing their tendencies, can overcome the problem and receive help. The partner should leave the scene before becoming a victim.

Parenting should be done with love, praise and simple discipline. The rules that apply to keeping house pets are apt for raising young children. There is not much difference in the antics of puppies, kittens and toddlers. They need to be kept warm and fed, as they can easily get lost or even injured; and they require some supervision. They must be told where they can go and areas that are forbidden.

Children will try to test their parents in order to gauge their own and their parent's strength. Strangely enough most children are quite happy when they know that they are loved and just how far they can go. When parents initially say, 'You can't do this' or 'You can't have that', and then break their own rules, it makes the child confused. This hypocrisy breeds contempt and both parties suffer in the long run.

You want to live a happy useful life. You want to be successful, to have friends and comfort. Purify your thoughts, visualise whatever you need. Don't covet the possessions of others. Make your thoughts positive and unique. Visualise, think and speak only good for others. 'Cast your bread upon the waters for you will find it after many days' (Ecc. 11:1). Good acts return beneficially to the sender. You must have faith in what you want and there are different kinds of faith. 'The Lord tells people that they are a perverse generation, children in whom is no faithfulness' (Deut. 32:20).

While out in a boat, a storm came up and the disciples woke Jesus to tell him they are perishing. He stopped the storm and asked them, 'Where is your faith?' (See Luke 8:22–25). A female sinner anointed Jesus' feet with oil. He told the others she had sinned much but had also loved much. He forgave her those sins and said, 'Your faith has saved you, go in peace' (See Luke 7:37–50).

Visualisation helps you in many ways – 'All things are possible to him who believes' (Mark 9:23).

Therefore imagine and see a picture in your mind of what you desire and it will come to you. This covers all areas and ranges from possessions, work and neighbours to receiving rainfall. The Great Spirit gave mankind dominion over all the earth (Gen 1:26), therefore we can also create, in our mind's eye, rivers, lakes and dams full of sparkling fresh water. Dominion was also given to people over fish, animals, birds and creeping things. Humans are the only objects who kill the former for sport.

Some also sacrifice animals and birds before the Great Spirit. As shown the creator produced it all from within himself. The Great Spirit is love itself and even gave us the commandment, 'Thou shalt not kill' (Ex. 20:13). Why then would one of these creatures be required to suffer fear, pain and death to absolve us from defects in our characters which only we are responsible for? Only we can alter our thinking and purify ourselves. In the past, mankind worshipped idols of clay, wood and stone. I would say that the practice of the sacrifice of animals came from this period. If you delve into archaeology further you can find that when civilisations dipped into their deepest, darkest periods they even sacrificed humans!

Let us talk about that personal final solution – suicide. Your higher self provided a blueprint which gave you an approximation of how you should live. It was approximate because your ego has free will. Your personality, looks, body, talents and faults were all collectively needed for this lifetime. There is a saying: 'You can perceive a glass with some water in it as half full or half empty.' This means you have either a positive or negative viewpoint. People do experience times when they feel low in spirits, 'Why are you cast down o my soul, why in me so dismayed? Hope in God for I shall again praise him, my help and my God' (Ps. 42:5–6). This is the time when you literally have to pick yourself up and try to be more positive in action, speech and thought. We all receive problems in life whether we are rich or poor. I prefer to call these challenges. I see 'problems' as hard and insurmountable, whereas challenges stir something within you and cause you to workout and overcome the difficulty. They strengthen you, fill you with elation and leave you ready to face the next. When you avoid facing a difficulty it will tend to surface again and again, usually in different disguises until you finally face and overcome it.

It's much easier to fall into self pity and become a victim of your own lack of self help than to live life itself which requires work, thought and effort. A tremendous lot of organisation has gone into providing you with this time frame in eternity. It's all in your hands to step into this body, grow and evolve and as you are not alone you aid others in their growth also. If you commit suicide, you the ego have directly disobeyed the higher self. Remember, the law of cause and effect steps in here. You have only put off facing those same challenges till a later date. Added to this is the sadness and sorrow caused to family and friends.

Know that you are never asked to do more than you can handle physically or mentally. You came into this world and are provided with everything you will require. There is a very enlightening psalm in the Bible (Ps. 23) which covers all the foregoing.

> The Lord is my shepherd I shall not want.
> He makes me lie down in green pastures.
> He leads me beside still waters.
> He restores my soul.
> He leads me in paths of righteousness for his name's sake.
> Even though I walk through the valley of the shadow of death, I fear no evil for thou art with me.
> Thy rod and staff they comfort me.
> Thou preparest a table before me in the presence of my enemies.
> Thou anointest my head with oil.
> My cup overflows.

> Surely goodness and mercy shall follow me all the days of my life and I shall dwell in the house of the Lord for ever.'

The meaning of this psalm is that my higher self protects me and provides all my needs. There is comfort and growth around. Emotions are tranquil. I learn about the connection of spirit and body. Like the prodigal son, I return home. I learn that death is an illusion. I have confidence because you are always there. Divine willpower and spiritual ideals give me hope. Support is always there even when I'm frightened, doubtful and cowardly. I am now dedicated for holy service. I have more divine resources than I ever dreamed were possible. Through possessing virtue and integrity, compassion and clemency will be extended to me and I will no longer need to return to Earth.

Some people long and wish for deeper spirituality. Finding this presents a challenge. Nature can provide us with a clue. There are trees which you can plant in your garden for shade. The nursery will tell you that they are fast growers. Some reach their mature height in only a few years. Their lifespan, however, is not long. They are not particularly tough and can perish in strong gales. Then there is the acorn. When it is planted, the tree appears to grow in a steady, unhurried, leisurely fashion. Its strong expanding trunk can hold many branches. These unfold a myriad of leaves, and it provides much shade, strong nesting places for birds, food from acorns and mulch from autumn leaves. There is longevity in oak trees. It is as though they receive as much as they give. People who wish for spirituality or psychic gifts quickly may use drugs, hypnotism or short cuts to open chakras.

Remember, if you receive a skill quickly it may be one which you can't handle properly. This can be confusing at best and can even lead to delusion or madness at an extreme level. Jesus said, 'Truly, truly, I say to you, he who does not enter the sheepfold by the door but climbs in another way, that man is a thief and a robber: but he who enters by the door is the shepherd of the sheep. To him the gatekeeper opens, the sheep hear his voice and he calls his own sheep by name and leads them out' (John 10:1–3).

This means that Jesus came as the teacher and gave us the precepts on how to live our life – love our enemies, treat others as we ourselves wish to be treated. We already hold within us the kernel of wisdom. If we meditate and seek within and use patience and faith we shall at the perfect time receive physical gifts and spiritual talents. Because we receive them at the right time we shall have the insight to handle them and the strength to use them. Understanding and knowledge shall accompany them. You will be on the spiritual path – you have walked every step to get there, you will not have hopped over a wall and taken your place like a thief or swindler.

There is a vast difference in being religious, psychic and spiritual. Religious people belong to a religion of their choice. They are asked to follow its dogma and observances. Most religions (there are a few exceptions) tell their followers that theirs is the chosen and only religion given by God. When they die they will be the only ones to go to heaven. Anyone not of their faith is lost, a heretic and most likely sent to eternal damnation. Within these religions are those with varying inclinations: some are fundamentalists, some follow a middle road and some follow it loosely, usually for a wish for peace and quiet from the community or family. The latter, to all intents and purposes, are hypocrites and living a lie. Psychics tend to have talents of differing kinds and may or may not be spiritual.

Those on the truly spiritual path will not advertise their way of life, but rather go quietly about their business. They are known by their deeds of kindness (usually undertaken quietly) and peaceful, gracious ways.

Clean up your thoughts and emotions, treat others as you'd like to be treated. Don't gossip or criticise, be loving and help others when required. Avoid laziness and learn to live in the present time – the now. As St Paul said, 'Behold now is the acceptable time; behold now is the day of salvation.' (2 Cor. 6:2). Start working on yourself right this minute. You may make mistakes; we are on earth because we are imperfect! We can learn through our mistakes, they are excellent teachers. Don't look back on the past, it can fill you with guilt. Set things in motion for the future, but don't live there, as it can fill you with fear, apprehension or worry.

Anyhow, events may proceed differently from what you expect! The present instant is the only space in time that you can truly focus on and live in. There is a verse (the origin of which is heavily debated) which I will quote: 'Yesterday is history, tomorrow is a mystery, today is a gift – that's why it's called the present!'

At this time the world appears a very exclusive place. A person feels better than their neighbour and vice versa. Families, groups, cities all appear to fall into this category. There is an old saying, 'All the world's a little strange save thee and me, and even thee's a little strange.' Most of mankind thinks that the Great Spirit makes them to be the only ones to finally ascend to heaven or paradise. Again I wish you to look at all items comprising the planet. It is made of dense matter but originated from the Great Spirit. Spirit life then is in everything – not just in mankind.

The rocks and earth are the lowest level as they arrived first. Scientists will tell you that they have found many sentient life forms. Therefore we can say that rocks and earth can know, 'I am' and feel heat and cold.

Following this there is vegetation. All components that I mention next possess the faculties of those lower in scale with the addition of further abilities. Vegetation would therefore add the feeling of fear, stemming from the proximity of birds or animals – would they get eaten? Pleasure would come also, maybe in the form of sunshine after a cold bitter period or welcome rain after searing heat.

In animals and birds, the spirit can take part in life on earth from various angles; under, on and above the planet. They possess rudimentary intelligence, the cunning needed to secure a mate, provide a home, raise a family and find food and water. If we as humans return finally to our source it must follow that they will do the same. The old concept of sitting in a white gown on a cloud and playing a harp for all eternity would, I think, bore most people!

If an ego on earth possesses ideals and views which may be good, bad or mixed, then surely it follows that the higher self would also possess ideals and vision of a higher order for its surroundings. Heaven would therefore contain mountains, seas and landscape which would continually please the eye. Vegetation and flowers would be perfect, perfumed and disease-free. Houses and public buildings would be of the finest quality and fit into their setting harmoniously. The lowest celestial area would have its regions devoted to the different races. You would want to join those races and colour you were most comfortable with just before you arrived. As we evolve and find out that race is unimportant, I imagine that higher heavens would accommodate spirits of all variety. Why then should it be difficult for some people to think that animals and birds would not populate the heaven worlds?

Animals and birds would be drawn to a realm visually resembling the terrestrial place they left behind. Also abandoned would be the ferocious side of their natures as they would now be in spirit form with no need to eat or drink. Those animals which were domesticated may wish to follow the same trend, and could you imagine a wood in heaven without the pleasant song of birds?

Death comes to us all in one form or another. When it comes to a baby or child it is devastating as in one way we think of the potential, imagined or demonstrated, which they revealed. A young adult has a similar effect when life is cut off. The death of the elderly is viewed in a more tolerant manner. Honest grief should be known and seen for what it really is. Those left behind are deprived of their company, their ideas, hearing their voice. In the end it is a purely selfish feeling. It is healthy and healing to grieve, but keep it short. It's not good for the spirit who has departed as the unhappy feelings of the moment reaches out and surrounds it when it should be free and untrammelled.

Lengthy grief is definitely not good for the ego or egos left behind as they can get drawn into a depressed state. Life must go on and the best solution is to plunge into some sort of work, paid or voluntary, until you feel the weight has lifted. You are not being selfish, you are giving the departed the freedom you would like when in time you, yourself pass on.

The education you receive this lifetime, child, is exactly what you require for your path in life. It is of no avail for parents to force toddlers with tuition. They think the child will miss out on being a huge financial success if they don't have it all now. We are talking here of those children who are born healthy and with no mental impediments. These children could be enjoying a period of years exploring and studying life and gaining perspective in many areas of existence. Getting in touch with nature and using their imaginations for invention is a must. Study of needed requisites can follow in a harmonious fashion. Even so some children are late developers who surprise everyone when they suddenly appear to blossom in some area of expertise. Those children who are born with or develop difficulties have come here to experience these challenges and need love and help. Mankind is mostly here to find wisdom in one way or another. To each person wisdom portrays a different face. To some it means how to obtain money and live an easy life, to others it signifies gaining expertise in sport, work, education or the arts. Wisdom in spirituality cannot be bought; it cannot be obtained through education or instruction in religion. It is a path which you decide once and for all to follow.

Someone said to Jesus, 'I will follow you, Lord, but let me first say farewell to those at my home.' Jesus said to him, 'No one who puts his hand to the plough and looks back is fit for the kingdom of God' (Luke 9:61–62). Meaning: don't procrastinate, start now!

Live in the now. Don't look back with guilt. You are a new person today. Books, workshops, churches can help some individuals, but in the end you must be quiet and listen to the higher self who talks to you from within. This we know is called your 'intuition' (teaching from within). Find yourself somewhere quiet where you will be undisturbed and sit quietly meditating. If you are the impatient type, start with ten minutes a day. Quiet, gentle music can cut out exterior sounds. You may like to burn incense but it is not really necessary. Ask for white light to pour into the room. There are also meditation tapes which you may find helpful. It's no use *trying* to empty the mind. Most people find this exceptionally difficult to do. We are a receiving station in our brains and therefore will be open to thoughts or trivial matters. Meditating is a discipline and requires the brain to focus on one area and stay with it. It would help to start your task by focusing on, say, a flower. Delve into it. How is it planted? What shape does it take while it grows? Look into its flowers, their colour and perfume. Take your time and enjoy the experience.

You may smell the perfume or find out something about the flower you didn't consciously know. Look into different items each meditation period until the exercise becomes easier to handle, and then you can delve into different emotions and why you possess them. You may find ways to handle them efficiently and overcome them. You can delve into past lives and how to manage present day associations. Allied to this, follow the guidelines the teacher gave when he said, 'Do to others as you would like them to do to you', and 'Love your enemies.' Start clearing out and cleaning up your inner self; only you can do it. Ask your higher self for help at all times, this is the true purification. Just think if you invited a very important person to visit your home and this person always wore white garments, you would want the house not only to look clean, but to smell fresh and look inviting. The same applies to your inner self; you must rid yourself of your base emotions and thoughts.

The teacher Jesus Christ can help you and you just have to ask him: 'Behold I stand at the door and knock, if anyone hears my voice and opens the door; I will come into him and eat with him, and he with me. He who conquers I will grant him to sit with me on my throne as I myself conquered and sat down with my father on his throne' (Rev. 3:20–21). Meaning: Jesus the ego went through trials parallel to ours. He overcame the temptations, met all challenges and triumphed. He was Christed. Now he takes on the task of supporting all those who wish to be helped.

The door is the opening portal of your heart and emotions. Once you open up to him, he can instruct you and you can digest the information. Your ego and higher self become as one and you will be enlightened and Christed. Most people on Earth see it as not a very good place at all and view heaven as a place 'up there somewhere'. We humans are like bubbles. All our own feelings, thought and emotions are held within this bubble. We also have the gift of free will. We can wake up in the morning with the choice of feeling happy or miserable. To be happy is to be uplifted so everything in your bubble is full of colour and joy. People are drawn to you like moths to a light. You are friendly and will have friends and help. Being miserable is a negative act, bringing harsh words and thoughts. Harshness is a harness which is heavy like rock. Weight pulls you down and so people avoid you, leaving you friendless and alone. Happy people then bring their heaven from within and surround themselves with it. Angry, grumpy people make their own hell and enclose themselves in this negativity.

Heaven, then, is a state which you the ego can bring through from the higher self. You don't have to wait until you die to pass into the heavenly sphere, you can experience it here and now, wherever you are and in whatever condition you may find yourself. An old saying covers this: 'Four walls do not a prison make nor iron bars a jail.' This brings you in full circle, the higher self working through the mind of the ego and the ego purifying all and reaching up, finding and knowing its God. Its goal, mankind's initiation: being Christed. Could this be the wonderful second coming with every eye seeing it?

But what happens, you may want to know, to those

spirits who are so ingrained in evil and will not alter, or who possess extremely powerful, wicked egos? Someone with a strong ego wishes to be noticed above all. We all require a strong ego but that which is needed must be disciplined and genuine and not corrupt. The worst that could happen to these evil ones is to be ignored and cast aside: 'And they will go away into eternal punishment' (Matt. 25:46); also 'They shall suffer the punishment of eternal destruction and exclusion from the presence of the Lord and the glory of his might' (2 Thess. 1:9). Meaning: 'They as spirits shall be stripped of every memory of the multitude of lives they ever owned and purified and cleansed until left in a pristine state where they would have to start afresh on life's journey.' The Great Spirit is love, not vengeance, and the spirit which flows from this source is perfect within.

My dearest grandchild, I hope I have covered most aspects of existence. I pray I have given you hope to live and experience life. I wish that I have imbued you with faith in higher ideals and the desire to follow them through to fruition.

Remember, we are all one…

References

Lamsa, George M, *Holy Bible from the Ancient Eastern Text*, San Francisco, HarperCollins

Lamsa, George M, *Idioms in the Bible Explained and a Key to the Original Gospel*, San Francisco, HarperCollins, 1985

Stevenson, Dr Ian, 'The Evidence for Survival from Claimed Memories of Former Incarnations', in: *The Journal of the American Society for Psychical Research*, April and July 1960

The Holy Bible, Revised Standard Edition, W M Collins Sons & Co. Ltd., 1971

The Kingsway Shakespeare, George G Harrap Co. Ltd., 1932

The Aquarian Gospel of Jesus the Christ, Levi, De Vorss & Co., 1979

Printed in Great Britain by
Amazon.co.uk, Ltd.,
Marston Gate.